EDITORIAL FREEDOM DESING

We love getting feedback from our customers. If you had the opportunity to give us a review we would greatly appreciate it.

thank you

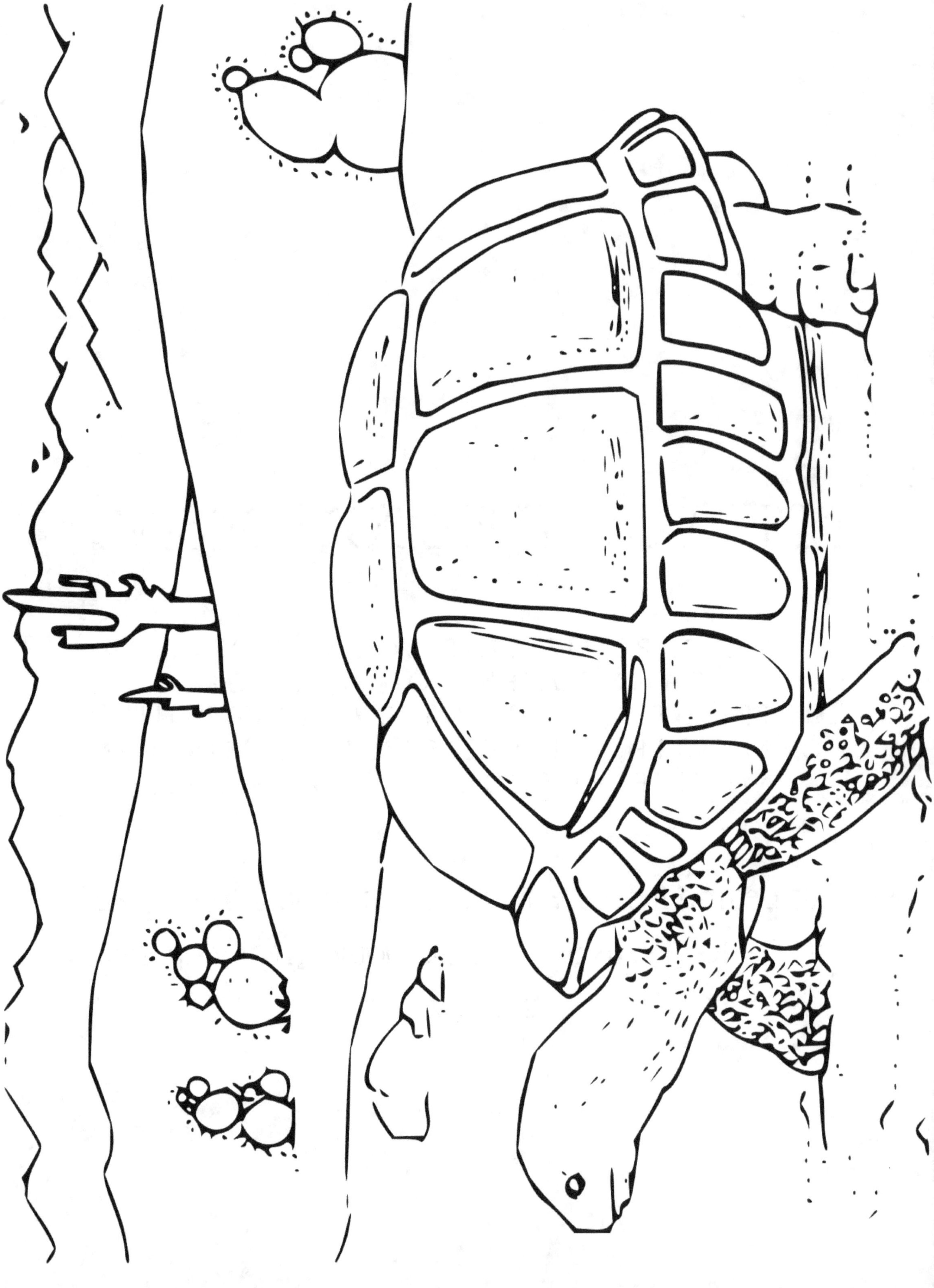

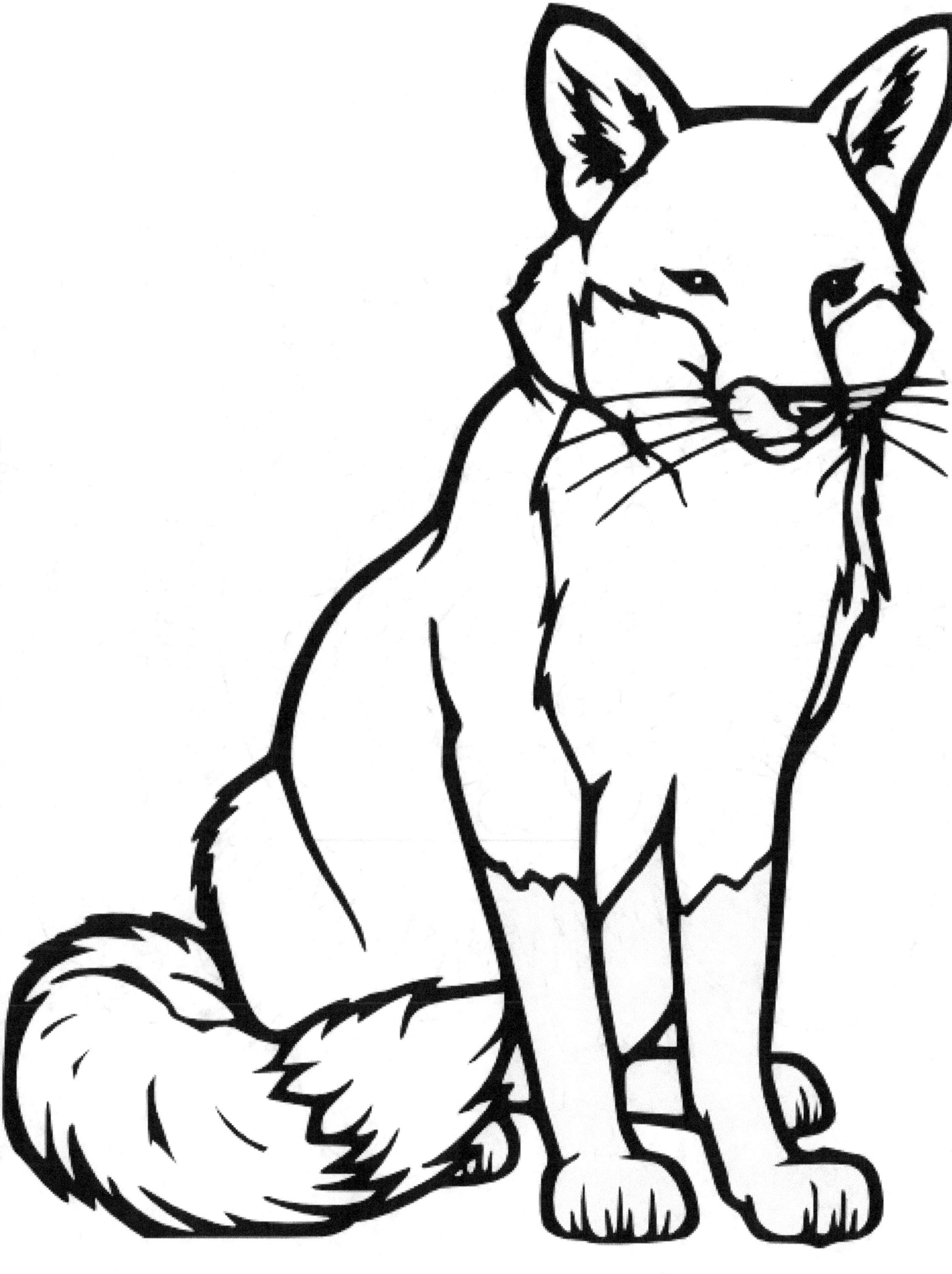

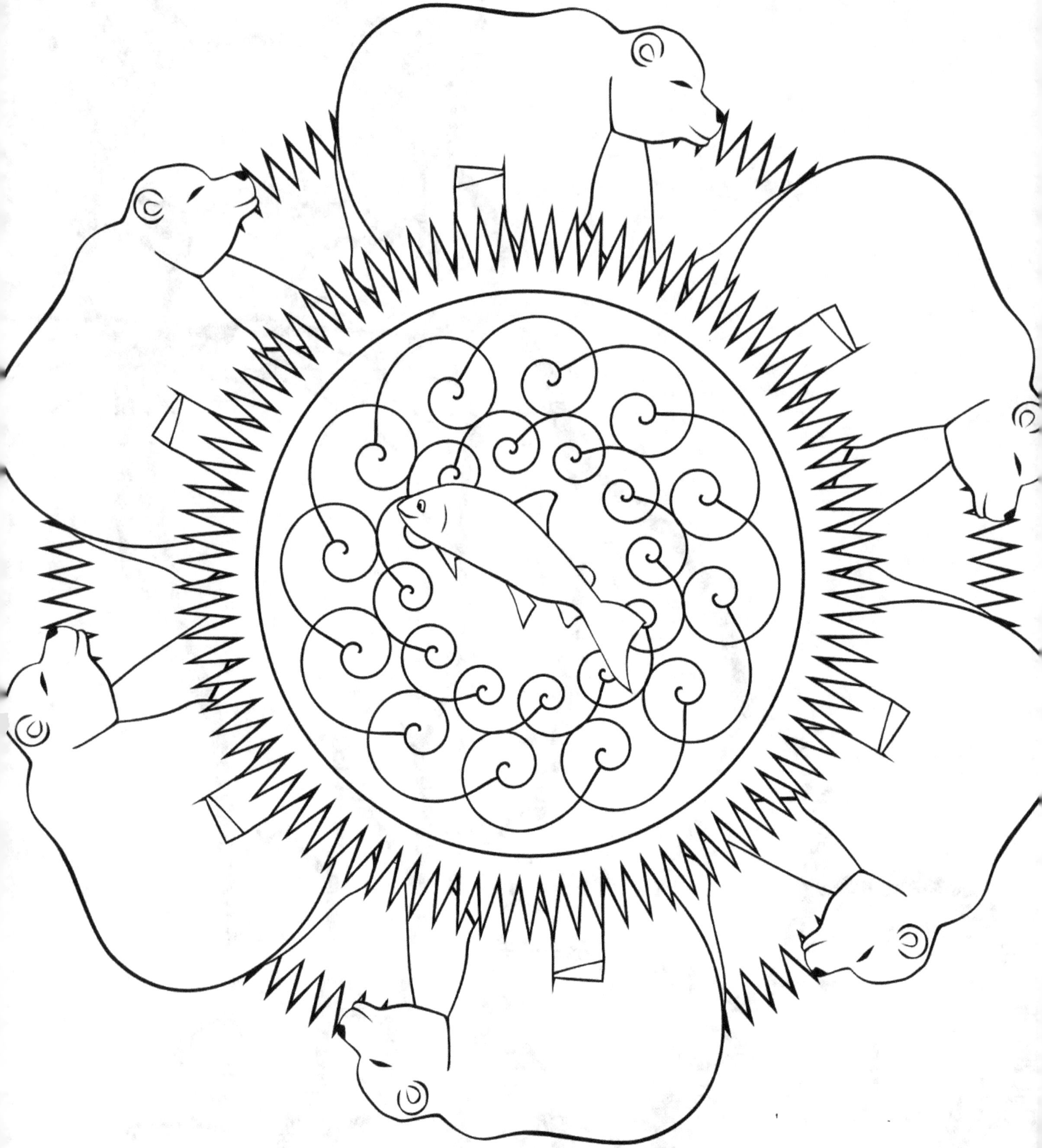

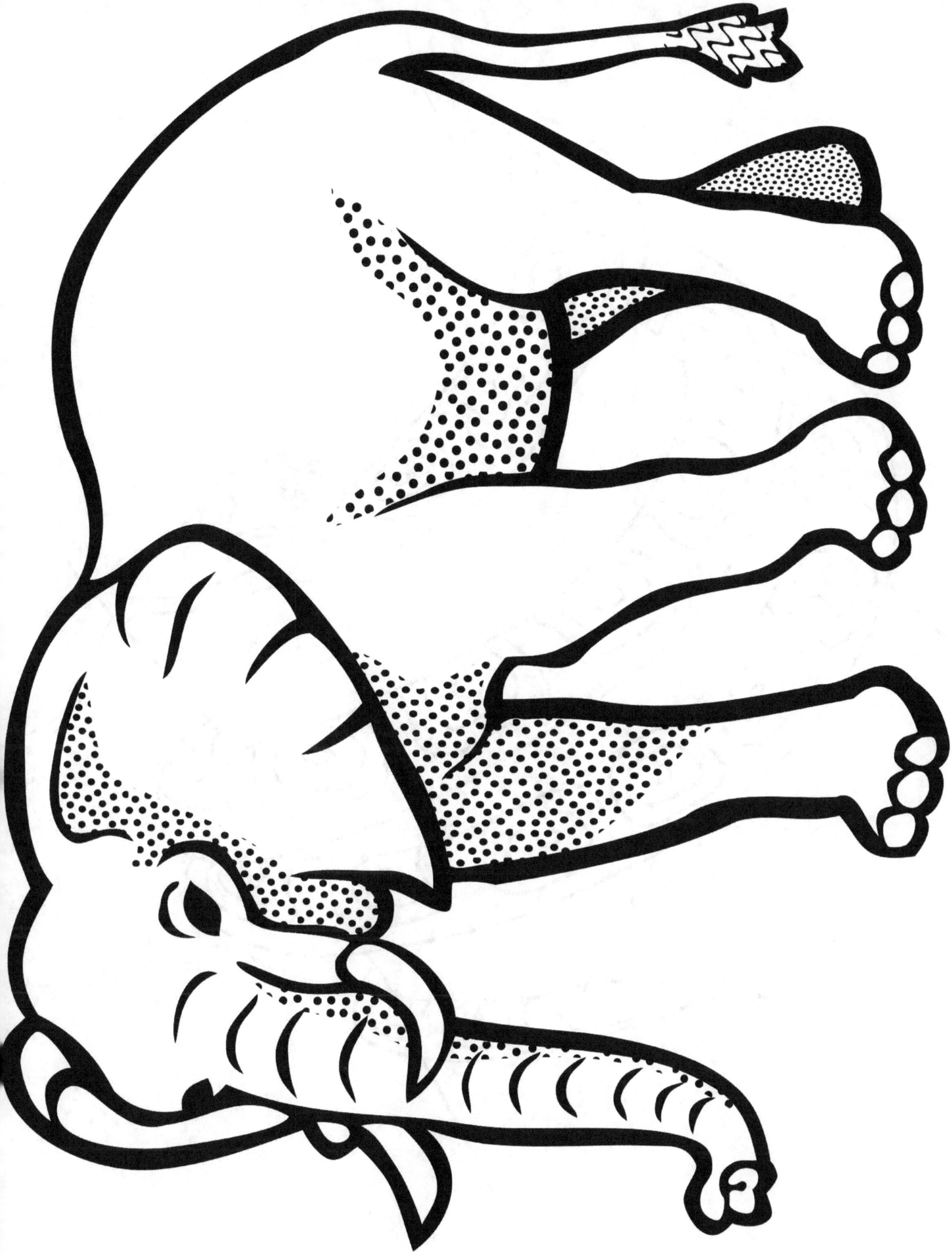

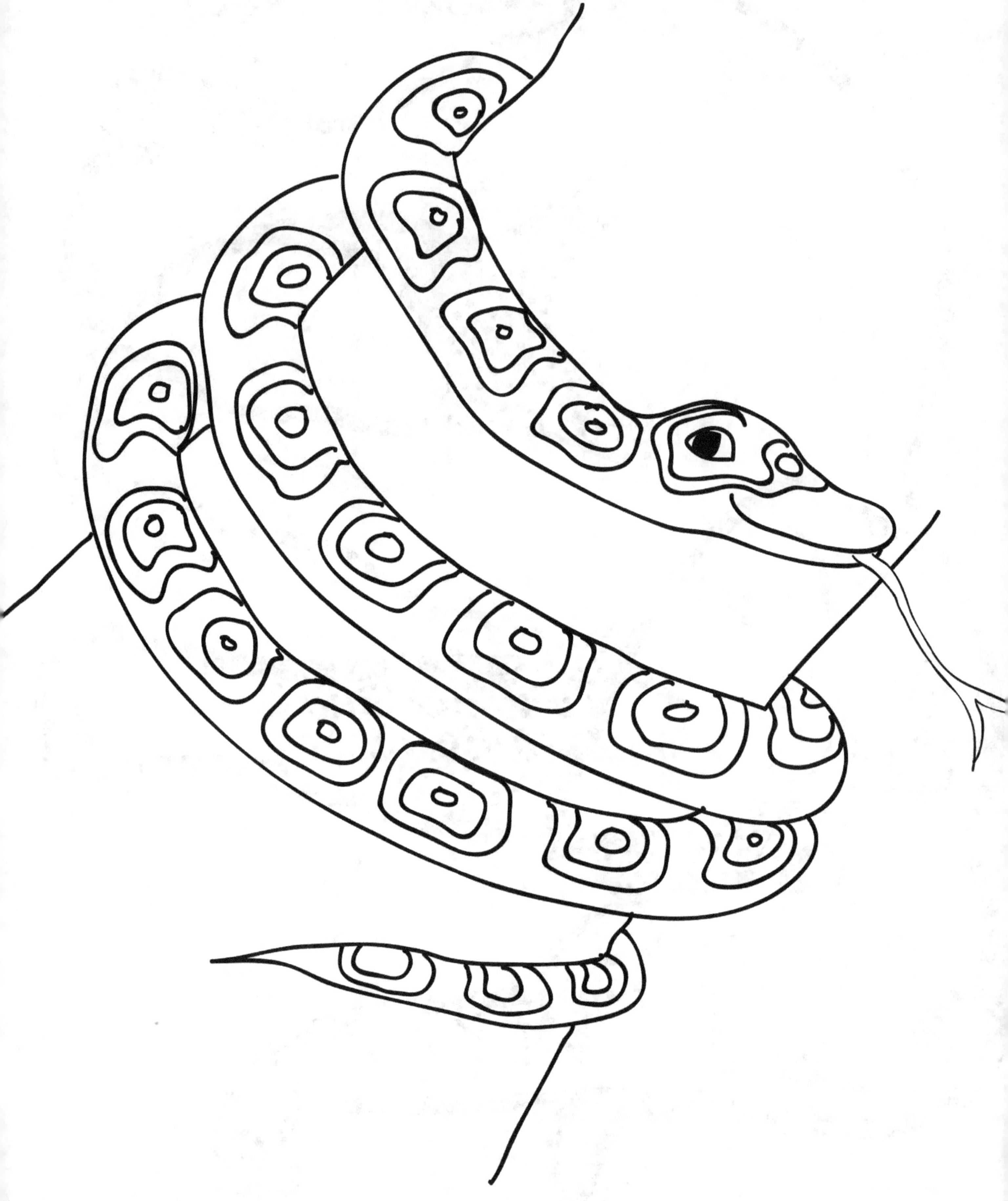

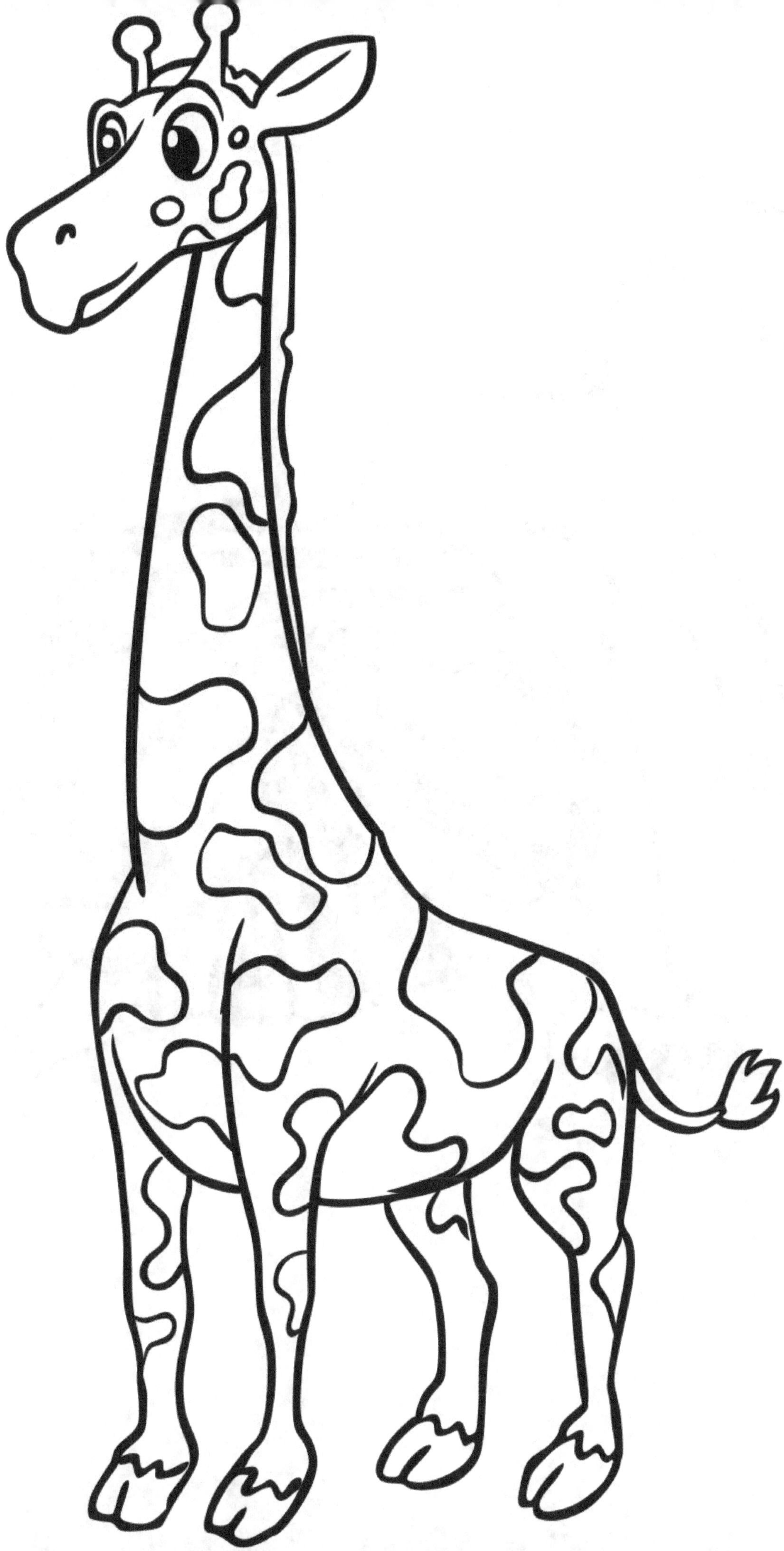

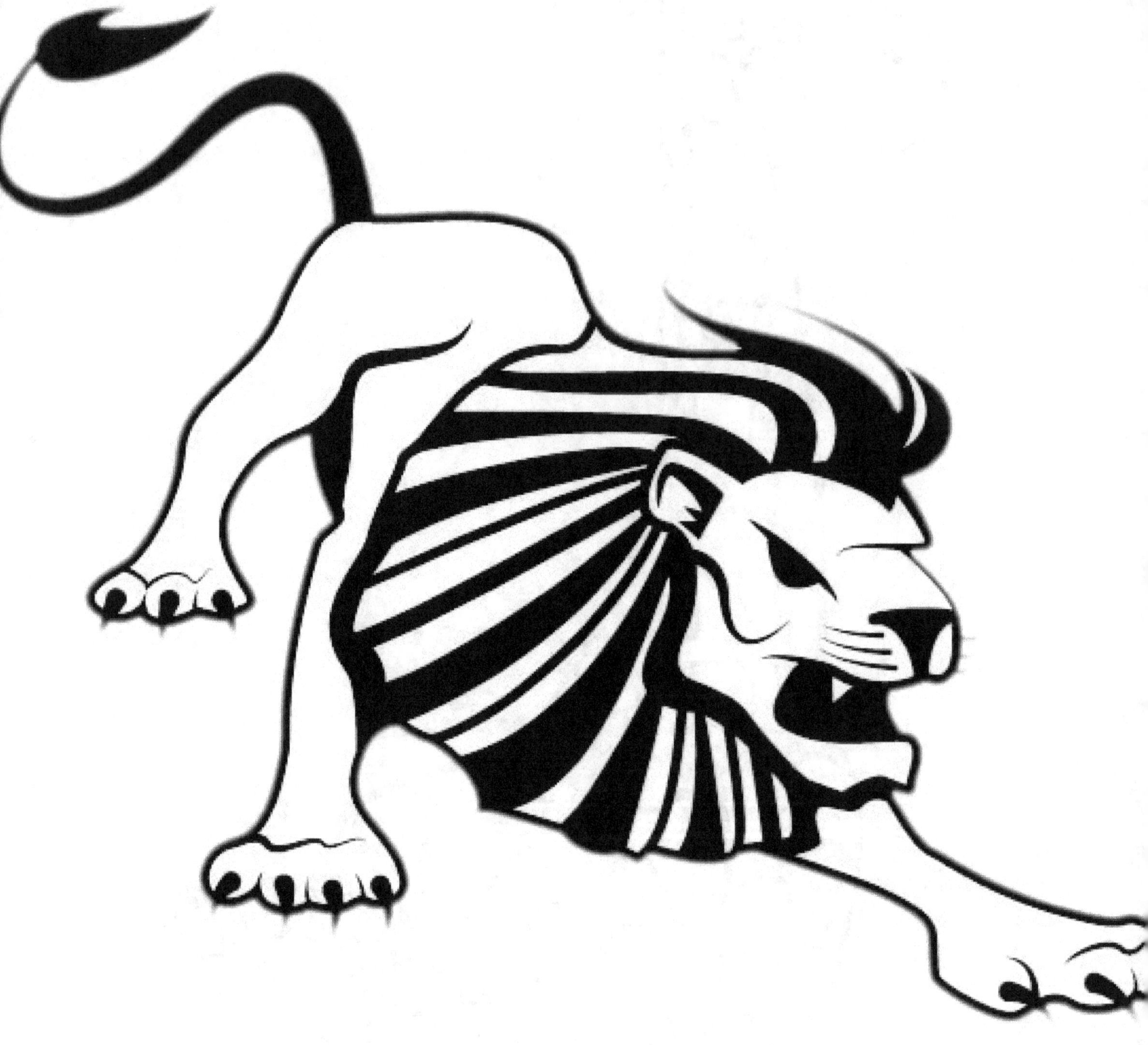

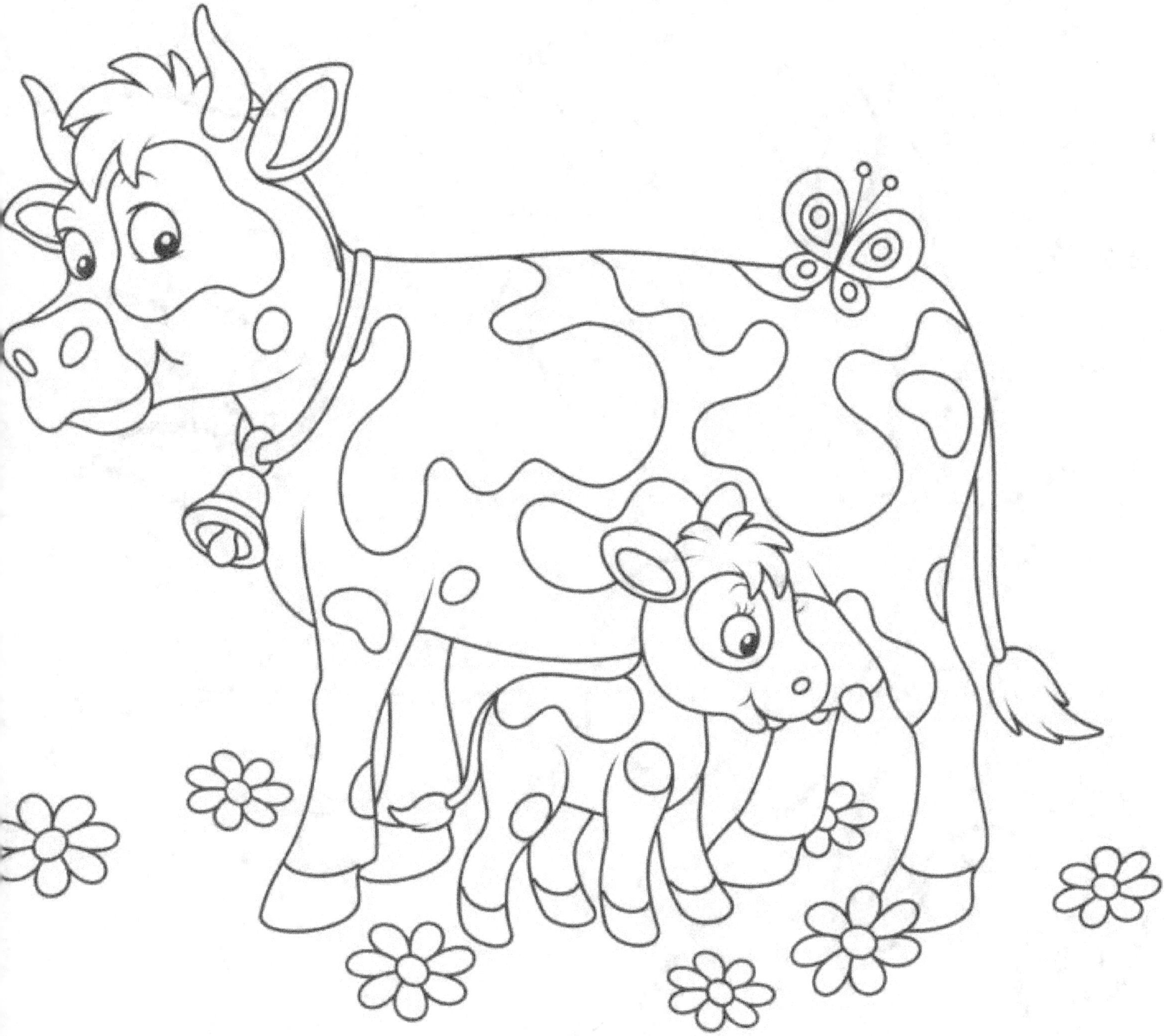

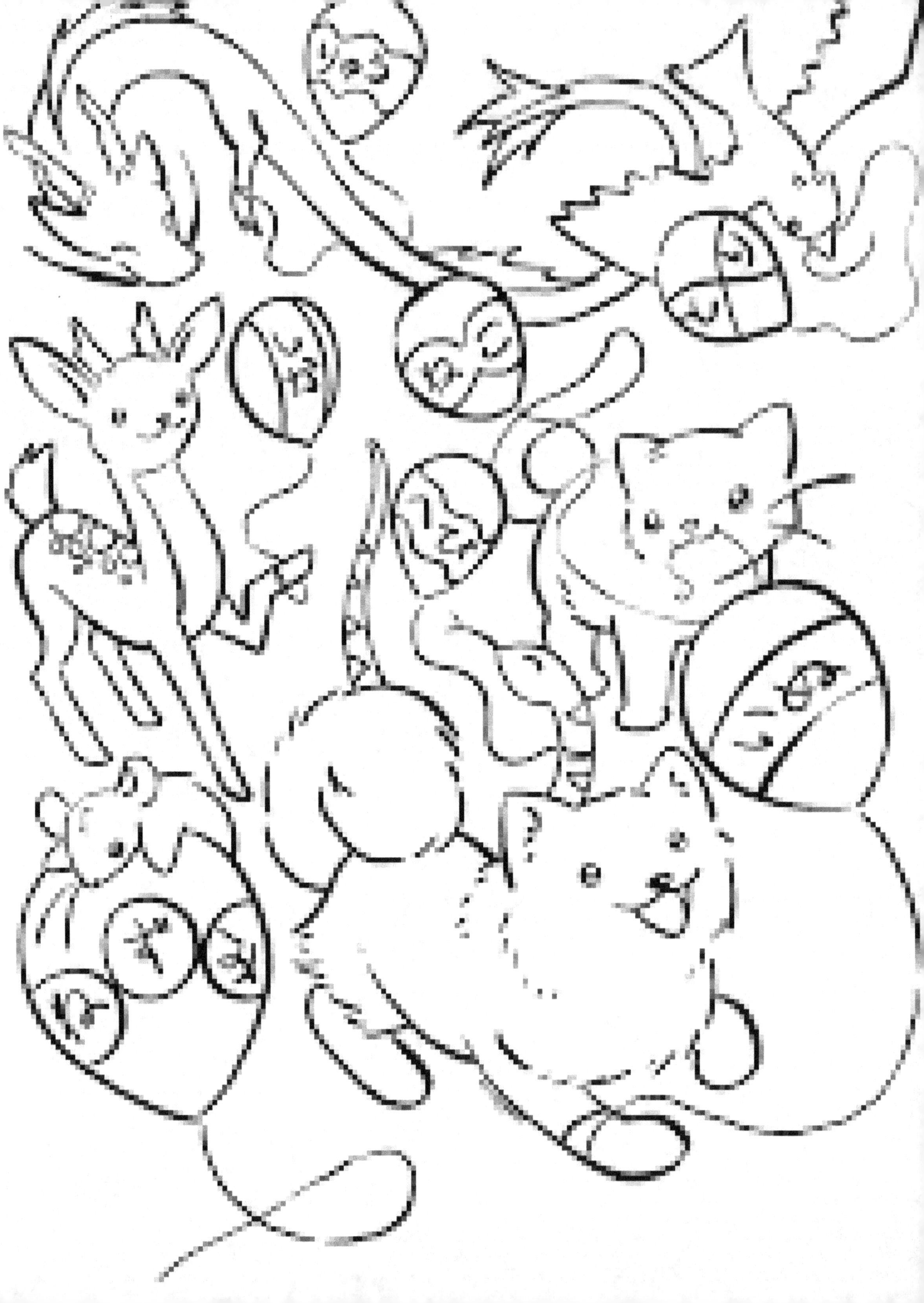

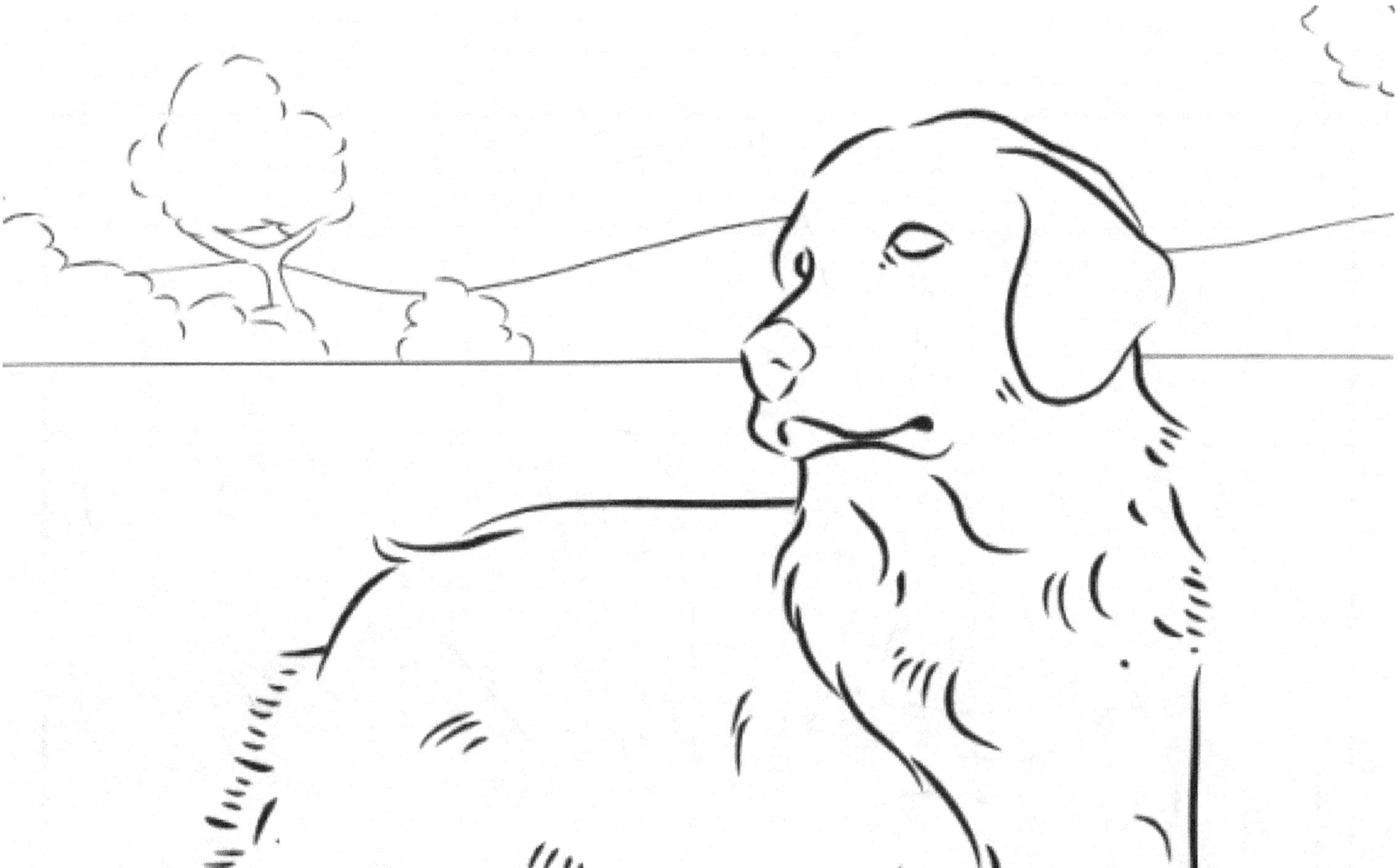

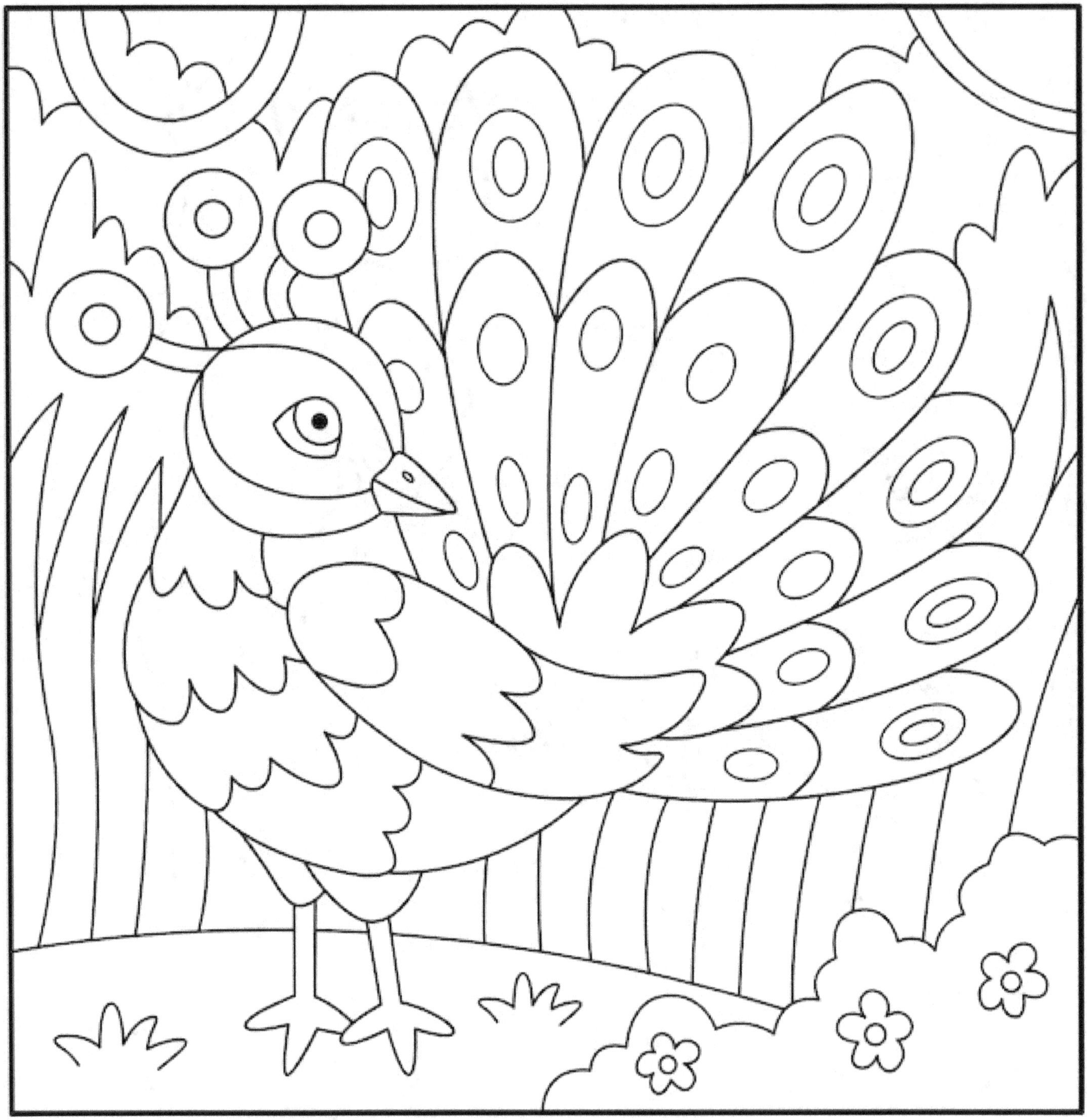

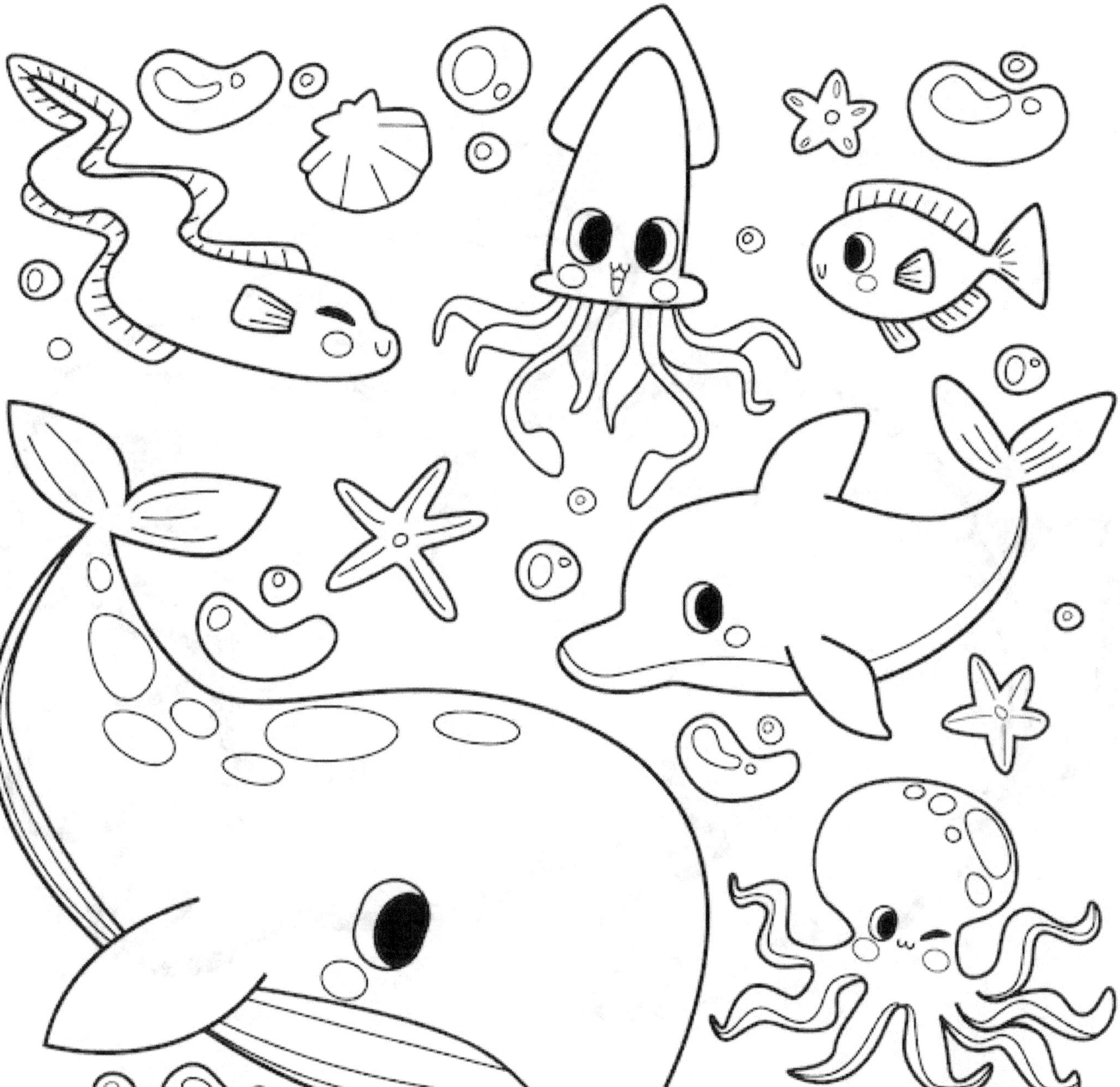

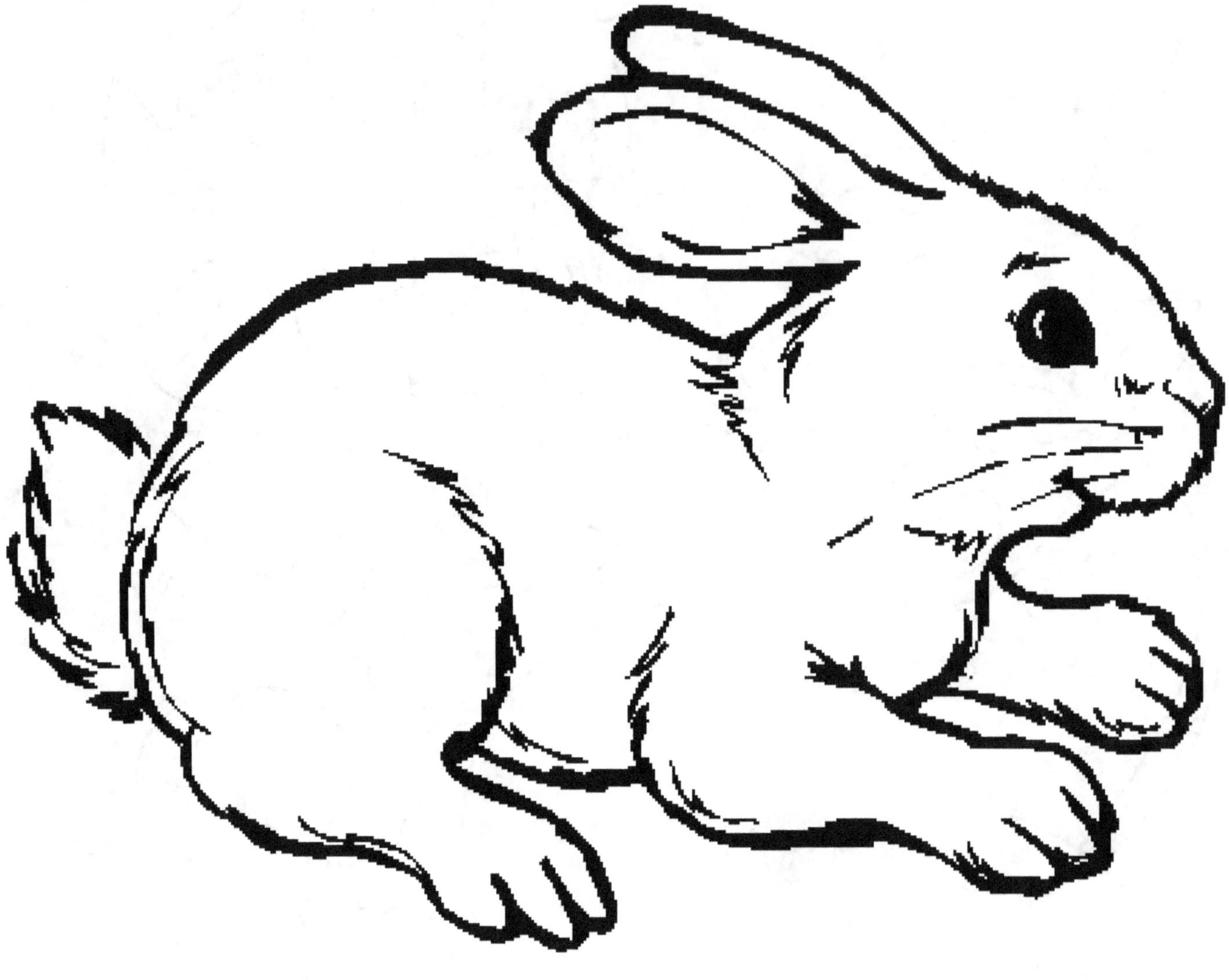

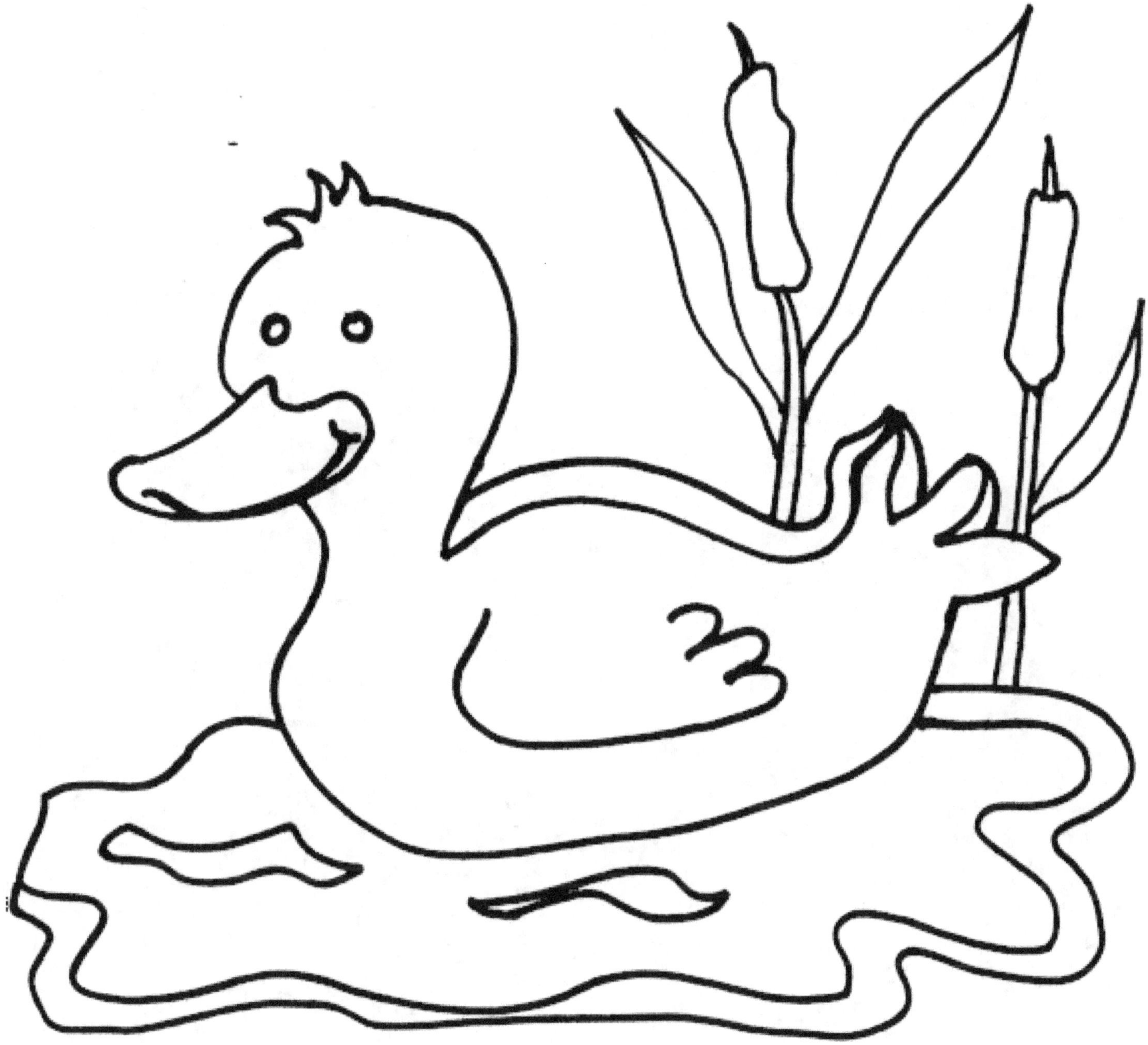

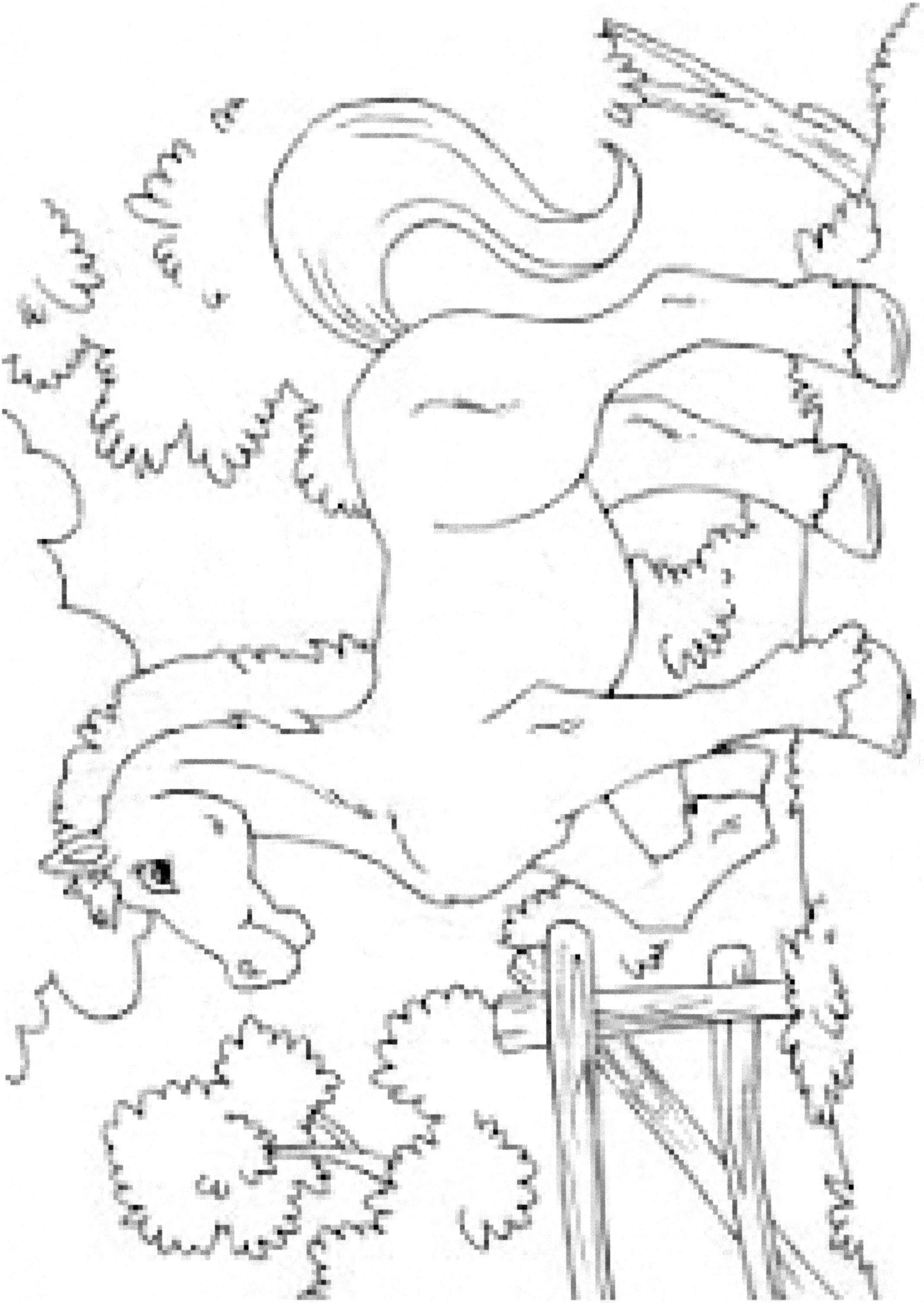

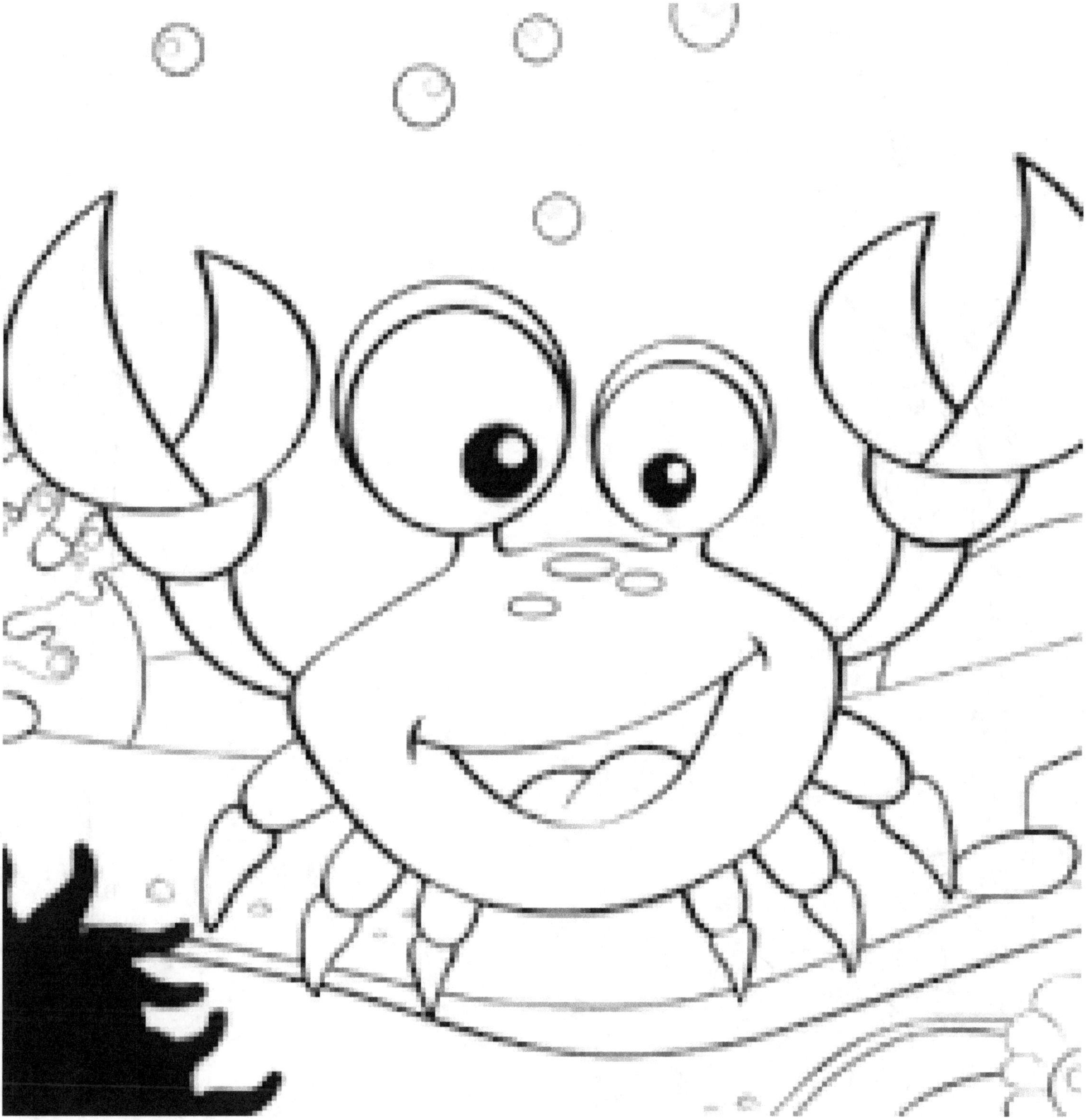

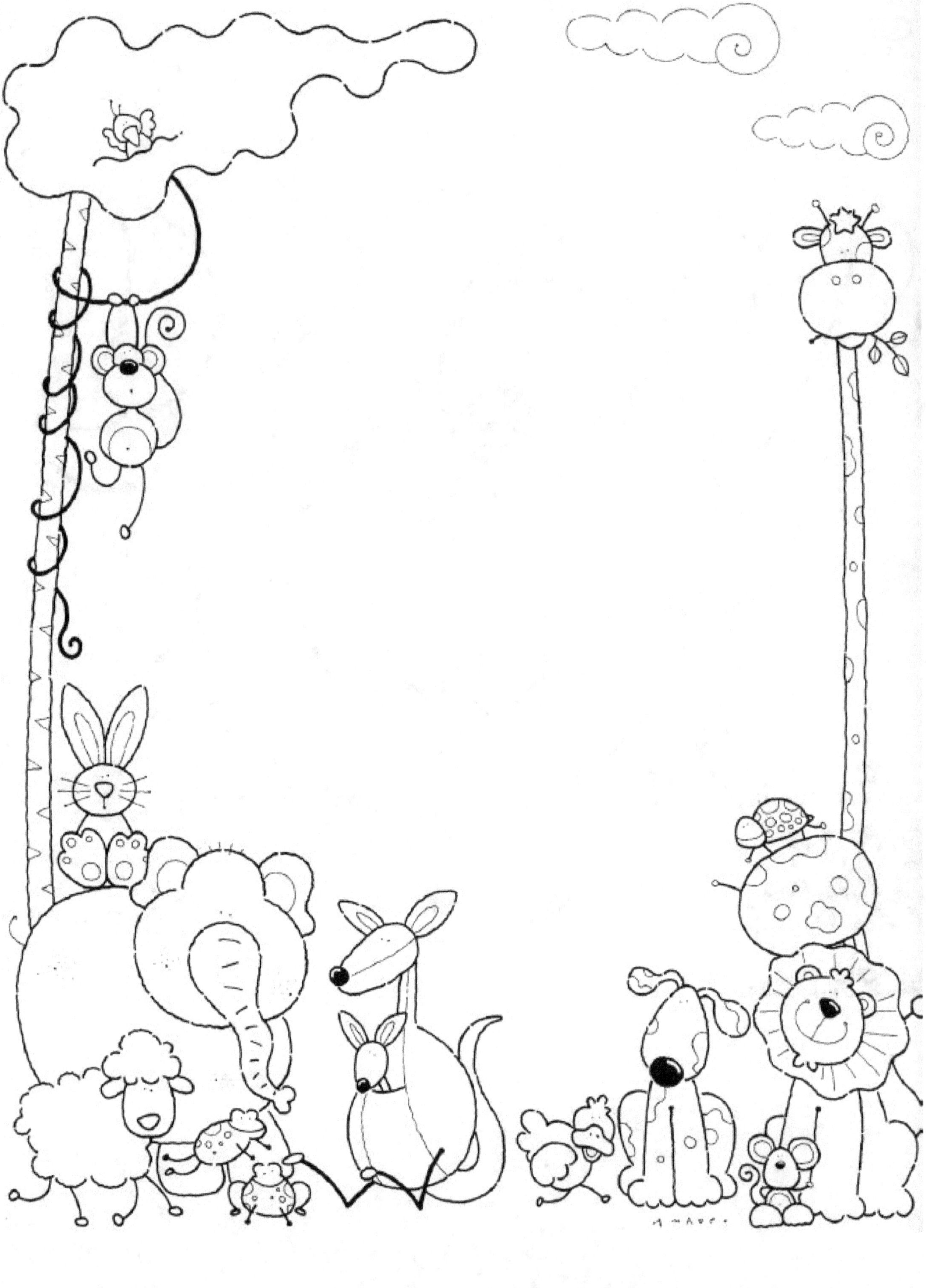

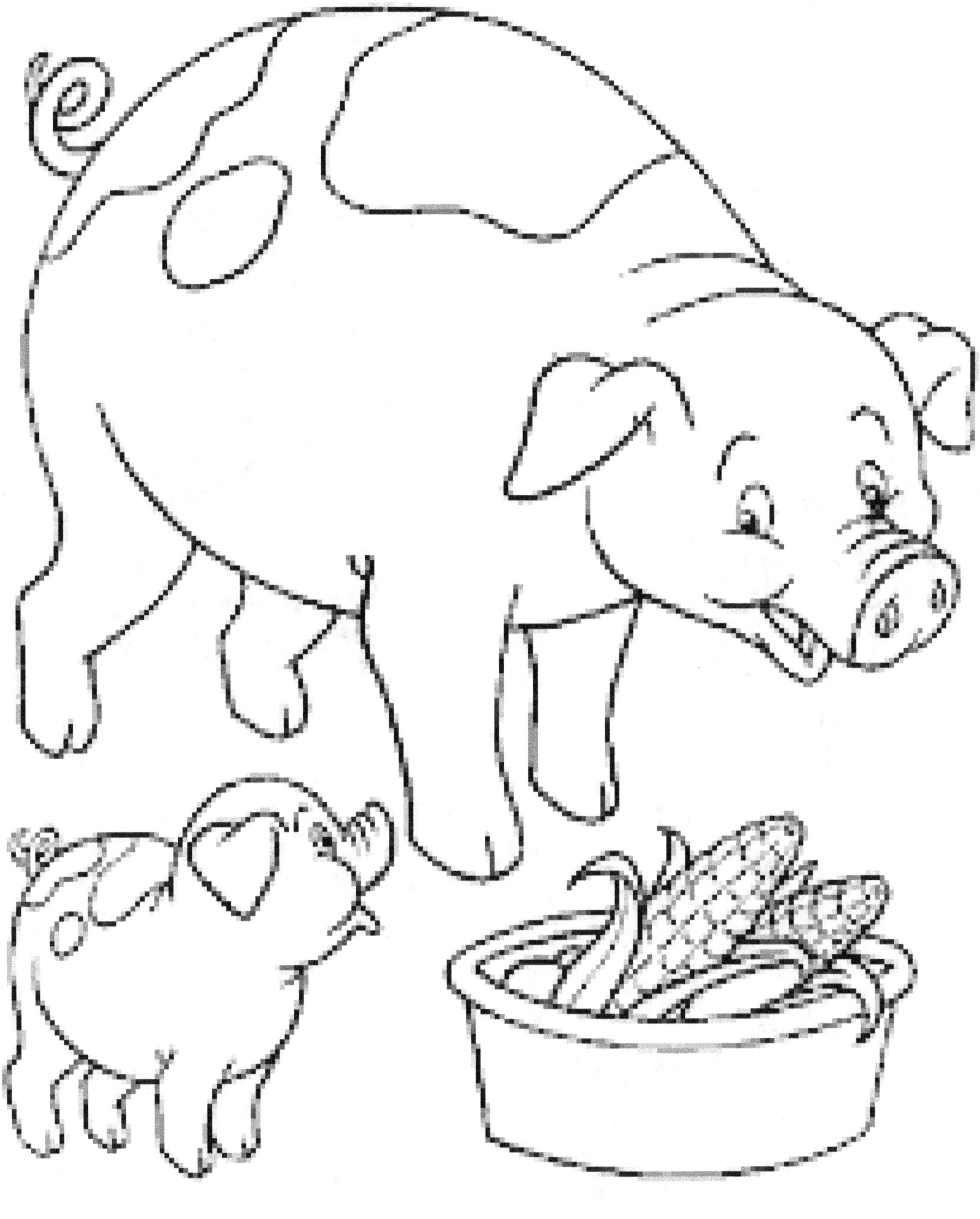

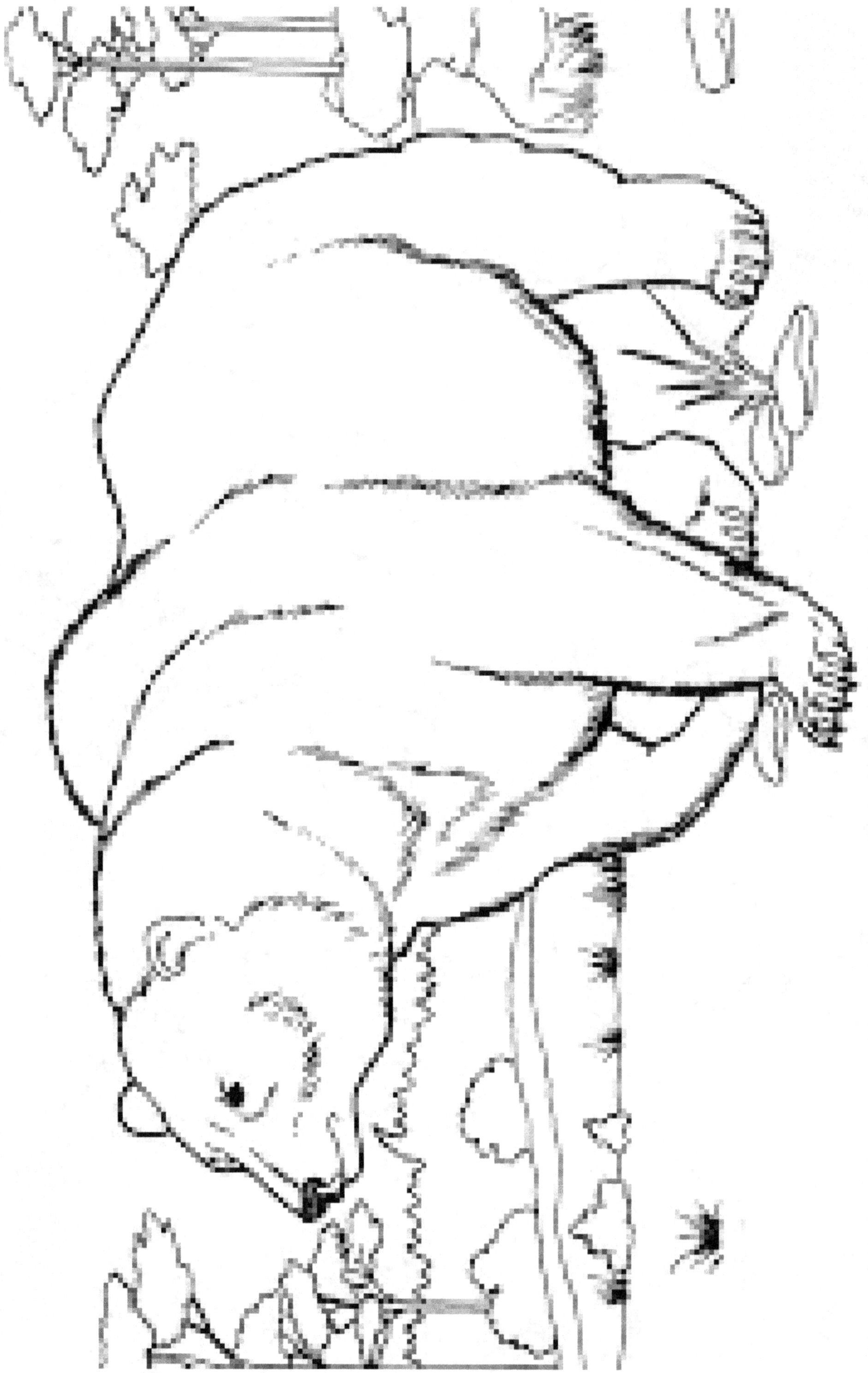

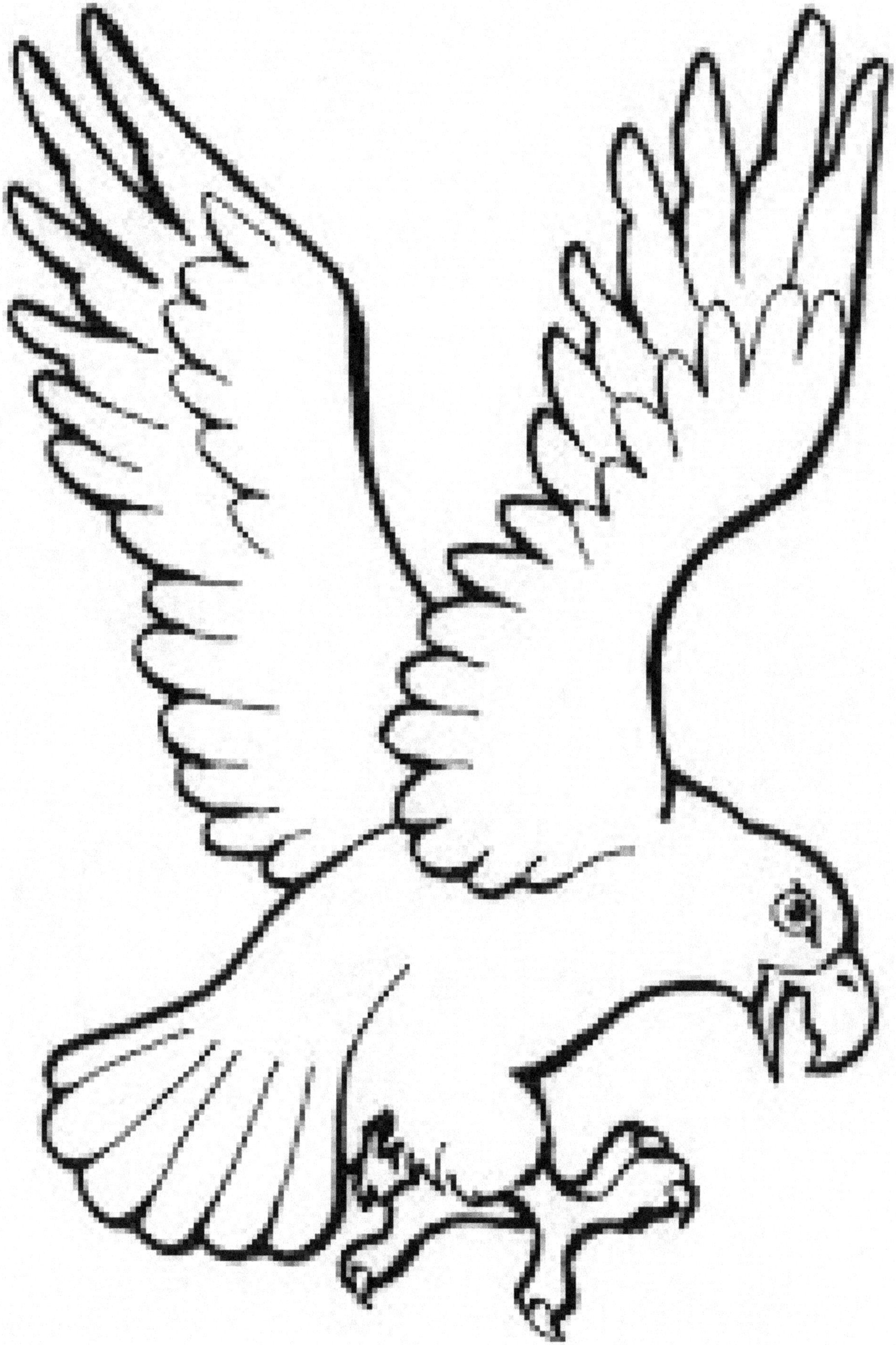

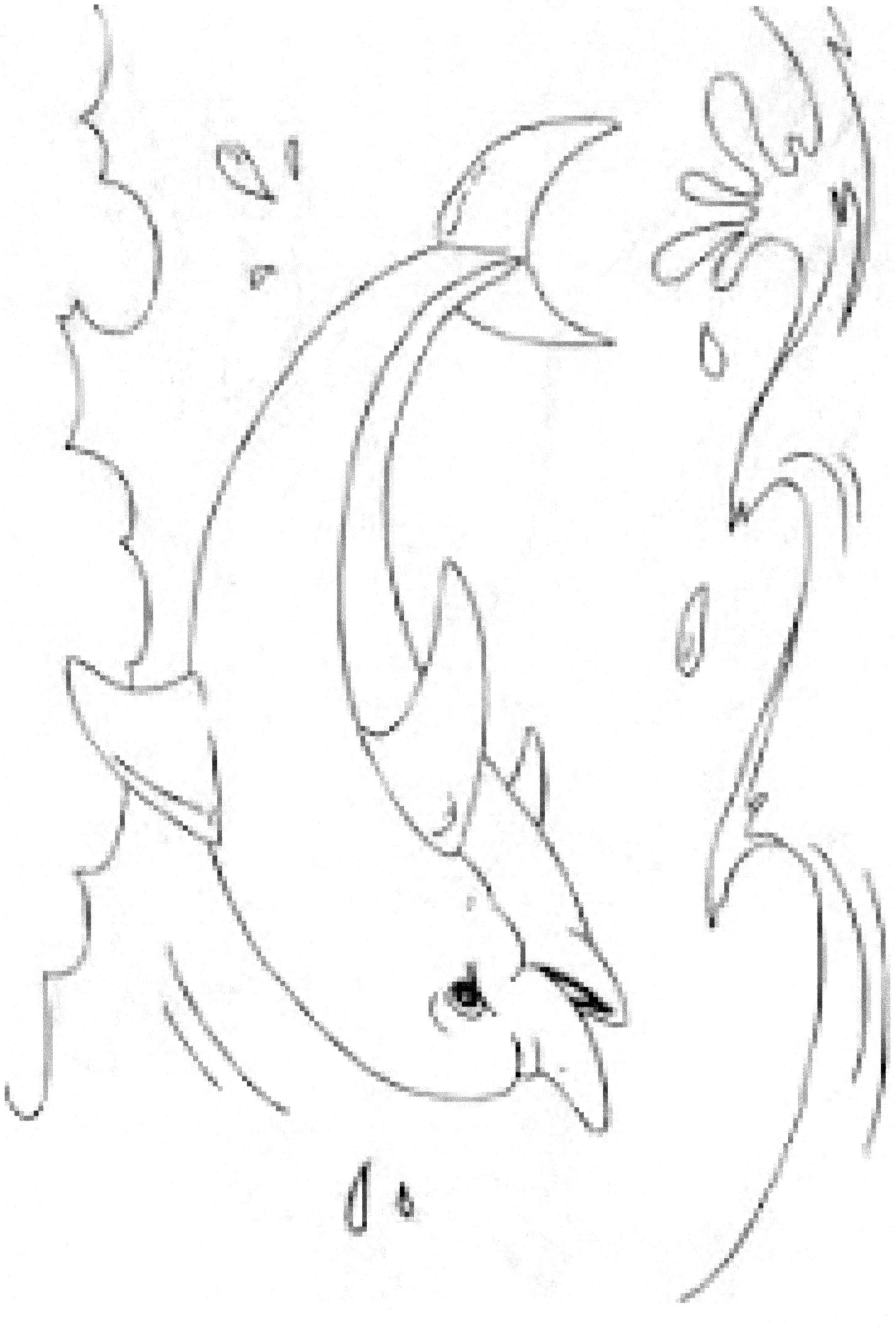

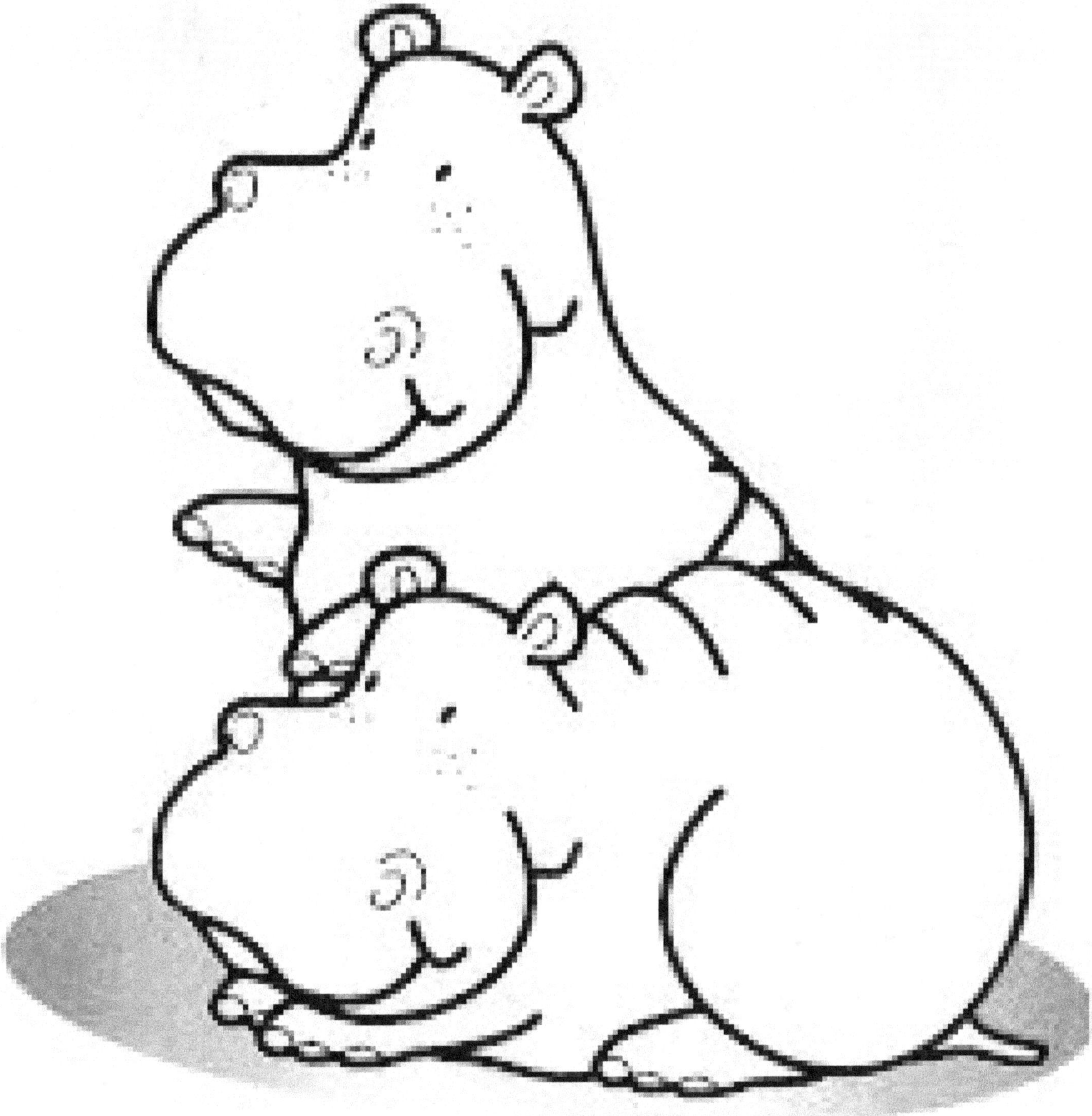

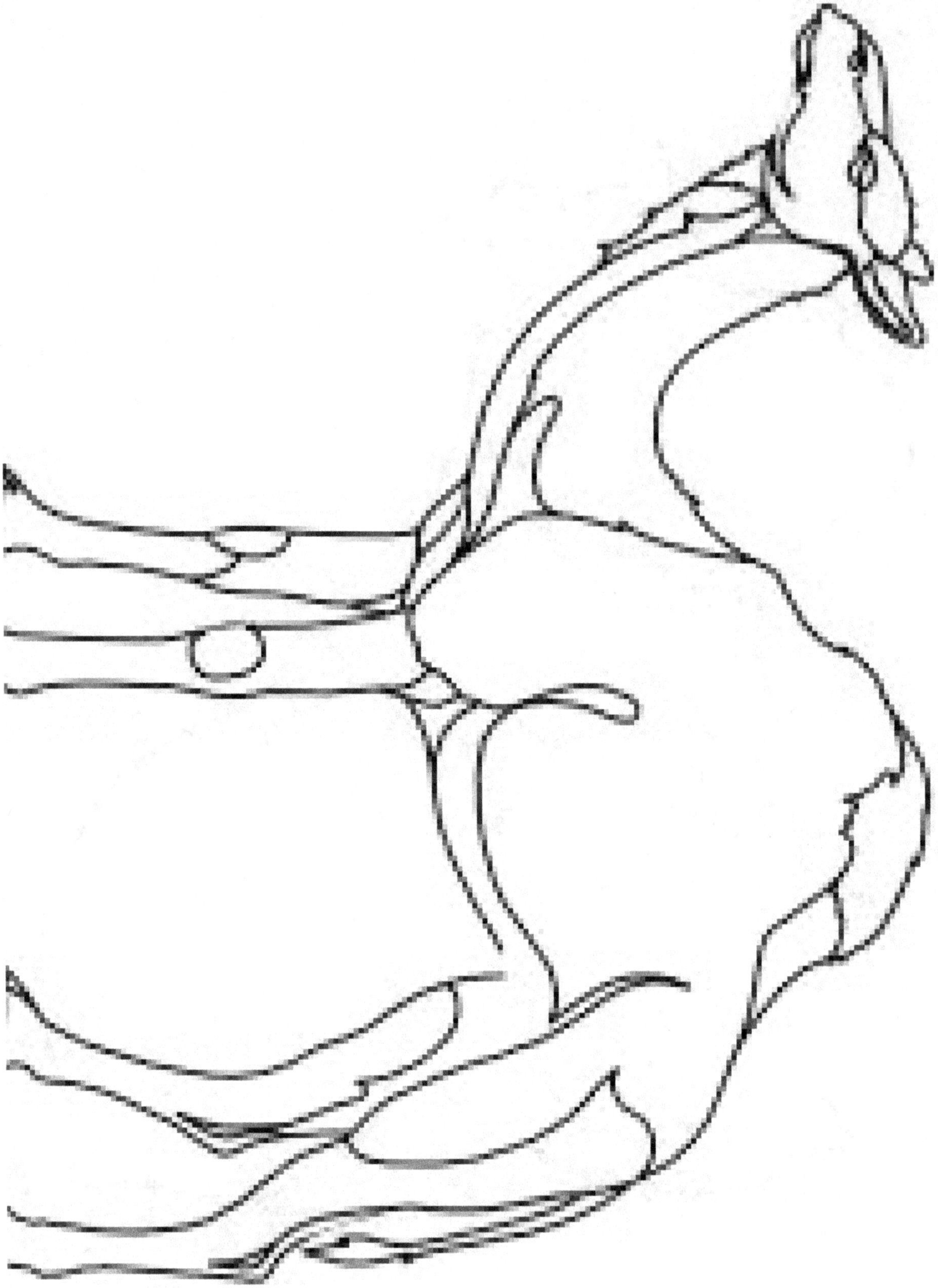

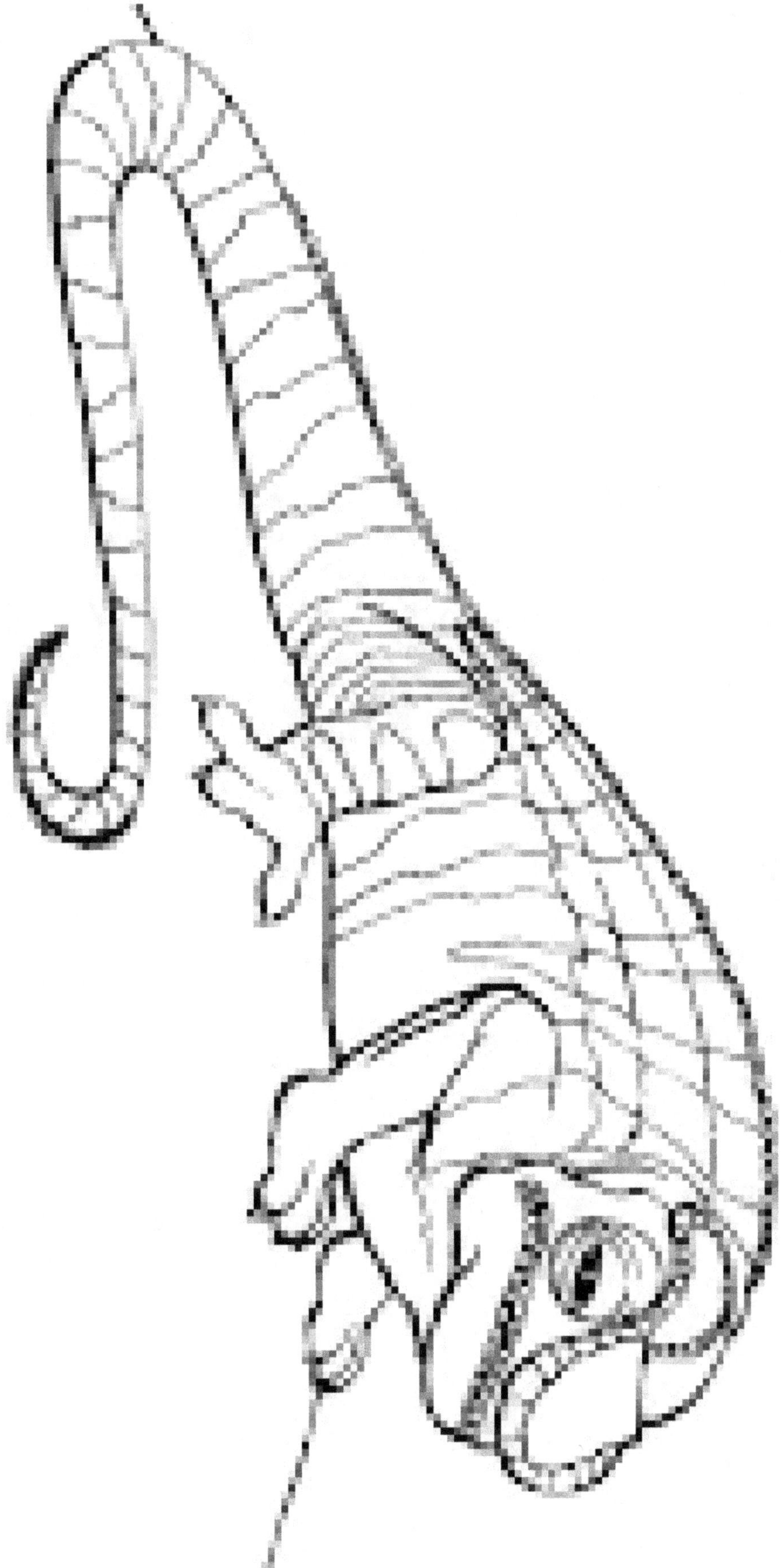

www.ingramcontent.com/pod-product-compliance
Lightning Source LLC
Chambersburg PA
CBHW080821220526
45466CB00011BB/3646
* 9 7 9 8 3 9 8 5 9 3 3 4 1 *